On Our Path

By

Gholamreza Rashidi
2025

© 2025 Gholamreza Rashidi Ardestani
Publisher: BoD · Books on Demand GmbH, In de Tarpen 42,
22848 Norderstedt, bod@bod.de
Print: Libri Plureos GmbH, Friedensallee 273,
22763 Hamburg
ISBN: 978-3-7693-5459-1

Dedication

To those who seek truth and meaning in the endless journey of life.

About Gholamreza Rashidi

Gholamreza Rashidi is not merely a seeker; he is an explorer of the unseen, a voyager charting the unmarked territories of the human spirit. Born in Iran in 1973, Rashidi embarked on his lifelong journey of discovery , dedicating more than thirty years to research and the study of mystical knowledge and the deeper truths within spirituality.

What sets Rashidi apart is his rejection of traditional hierarchies in spirituality. He boldly challenges the notion of leaders on the spiritual path, emphasizing instead the innate potential within each individual to uncover their own truth. To him, the universe is a unified whole, a vast and interconnected "blockchain" of understanding and consciousness. In this network of unity, any new idea or hidden secret explored by a true seeker is automatically shared throughout the entire system, enlightening all who are ready to receive it. This revolutionary doctrine highlights the boundless capacity for human beings to grow collectively, without the need for external intermediaries or guides.

Rashidi's writings are not teachings in the conventional sense. They are windows into his personal experiences, offered not as instructions but as inspiration for others to embark on their own journey. His works—ranging from poetry to philosophical dialogues between teacher and student—capture the depth of his understanding while inviting readers to forge their own paths.

In this latest book, Rashidi shares his profound insights on the mystical path, offering readers not a map but a spark—a reminder that the journey is theirs to define, and the discoveries are theirs to claim. He writes not to guide but to illuminate, not to preach but to inspire.

This book is a voice for those who dare to seek, a companion for those who dare to question, and a reminder that the greatest truths lie within.

Table of Contents

A Word to the Reader

The promise of immortality offered by religions never satisfied me; they lacked sufficient reasoning. Despite their seductive promises, they caused more death and constrained the brief span of life with countless restrictions.

I could settle for nothing less than immortality. Without it, every meaning, every effort, was hollow and futile. It seemed as though no one took death seriously, despite its inevitability.

I set out alone. The boundary between slavery and freedom is razor-thin—like a single breath: one, two, three... and then it's over! Move forward! Come what may!

It seems to be the same for everyone. The comfort of habit has dulled our courage. We don't pursue freedom; we live the habit of servitude as though it were life itself.

On the path of misguidance, I walked straight toward guidance. I realized I neither desired to seek the right way nor to avoid the wrong one, for when all paths led to the same destination, there was no escape, no diversion. No Turkestan. No Kaaba. No desert. No garden. There wasn't even a "me" to traverse the path. Whatever existed was a series of occurrences:

An endless becoming. A continuous losing oneself in an infinite expanse.

There was no one to ask, no one to question. No question existed. No answer existed. All there was—was an event within nothingness, and that nothingness was tangible to no one.

Yet, at the furthest point of misguidance, in the realm of the saintly irreverent, truth revealed itself more clearly than anywhere else.

I could have become the leader of a world. I could have founded a new creed entirely built on misguidance yet rooted in a pure truth. I could have sparked an upheaval from serenity, alongside the damned clothed in sin. Or, none of these could have happened, leaving only an event—a moment of nothingness—and that would be the end of it.

There is a boundary, crossing which places you on a one-way path. Everyone has the opportunity to cross this threshold, but not everyone does. For those who do, their world collapses. They win a chalice, drink its wine, and thereafter no other drink can quench their thirst but that wine.

That thirst drove us to madness, yet we refrained from touching the chalice—until one drop trickled down our throats, igniting a flame that even the angels fled from. The interval between thirst and that ignition was a season of intoxication, recklessness, and disbelief in every doctrine. It was a dead end in the most boundless expanse without walls. It was a descent into annihilation, into nothingness, into madness, into unbelief. And then, in one moment, a single drop would fall again, wings would flutter, and an ascension—of the kind born of utter self-forgetting—would begin.

You, who the entire cosmos has conspired to bring to this moment, to read these words, I am speaking to you. If nothing satisfies you, if you're drowning in nothingness, madness, despair, and disbelief, perhaps, without realizing it, you have crossed that boundary!

The drop of wine that can turn you into a blazing flame is with me, and I am not stingy in offering it. The solution is simple: align yourself with whatever is possible— nothing more, nothing less.

Yet, in this writing, I have spoken in the most cryptic manner, for I refuse to close the door to imagination. I consider myself bound to keep that window open, for everything—seen and unseen—reveals itself beyond this window. Each time you look with fresh eyes, you discover something new.

The Realm of the Journey

Where there is silence, light and darkness are one and the same. I could explain this to each and every person willing to listen, but I choose not to speak. I do not teach anything. Instead, I expand something intangible so that those who are true seekers may experience it for themselves—without the need for words.

It doesn't matter where in the world they are or in what era they live. Time and space are properties of the material world; they do not affect meaning. I extend meaning itself, though to call this "extending meaning" is itself an uncertain term. Meaning is infinitely expansive. What must be expanded is the human capacity—to enable one's inner being to host ever greater depths of meaning.

In doing so, something passes through me. And as it flows, I, too, pass through it, reaching new frontiers. This is an irreplaceable benefit. I, in turn, have benefited from what others have expanded before me. It is an endless, timeless exchange.

To encounter meaning is to confront infinity—and the human body cannot bear it. Humanity is finite. One must understand their limitations and gradually expand them. There have been moments when, merely in the proximity of meaning, not even fully immersed in it, I have seen everything fall apart. The safe island of human existence seems to suddenly sink into an ocean, vanishing as though it had never been.

Neither logic, nor feeling, nor illusion! And yet, all logic, all perception, all imagination! Words simultaneously hold meaning and contradict themselves—contradiction within meaning, and meaning within contradiction! Chaos within unity, and unity within chaos. I have no better way to describe that state.

Our world is a world of opposites. It is the interplay of contradictions that makes the concept of the world intelligible to us. Likewise, on the path of spiritual growth, opposing perceptions drag the human soul into an unrelenting battle.

I remember a time when, overwhelmed by the hardships of the path—the loneliness, the seemingly fruitless struggles—I wished for death. I also remember a time when the joy and ecstasy of each new station intoxicated me so deeply that I would have traded my life to extend those moments. Both were forms of self-sacrifice—but oh, how different they were!

I know people who have been driven to despair by the grinding monotony of everyday life without even engaging in any spiritual journey. Yet, I believe the path I've walked—even if it were a misstep—was worth taking a thousand times over.

I also firmly believe that no seeker has a duty to guide others. Those who believed themselves tasked with such a mission polluted the world, killed and were killed, dragging opportunities for growth into the abyss of annihilation. Their hollow slogans sanctified death, skillfully dressing it up, while promoting violence and martyrdom. Spilling blood and dying only make sense in the service of a bloodthirsty deity.

Teaching is not my task on this path. Perhaps my task is forgetting. But even that is not quite right—there is nothing to teach, nothing to forget. Whatever I wish for, I simply say, "Let it be," and it manifests. What appears, however, is but an impermanent illusion—a fleeting reflection of the infinite manifestations of meaning. Even if there were a thousand galaxies within a thousand galaxies connected by a thousand paths, they would all still be illusions.[1]

Some people suffer even in these illusions. How astonishing! They are trapped in habitual patterns

---

[1] Writer is saying that teaching others is not their focus on the spiritual path. Instead, they believe that their true task might be to forget everything—forget ideas, labels, and teachings. However, even this idea of forgetting is not exactly right, because, in the end, there is nothing to really teach or forget. You just to be open to everything as new.

They explain that instead of trying to change others or the world directly, they simply focus on themselves and say, "Let it be," allowing what they want to happen to manifest naturally. However, what manifests is only temporary—it is like an illusion, a brief reflection of deeper, infinite truths.

The writer goes on to say that even if there were countless galaxies and paths in the universe, they would still be part of this illusion. True change happens within, and by transforming ourselves, the world outside will change too.

within their illusions. When a person steps away from the aimless wandering of mundane life and sets aside their trivial desires, they may realize clearly what they do not want—but they still do not know what they truly want.

As long as past habits govern them, they will continue to arrive at destinations they do not wish for. Nothing will change on this path until those habits are broken.

I have tested many people. When they find themselves in a mental deadlock, unable to make new decisions, they surrender their will to instinct. Instinct is the same force that drives animals. This is why the training of animals relies on reward, punishment, and conditioning.

Humans do not have patience. They often wait. Waiting is a painful and exhausting process that eventually wears them down, forcing them onto a different path. But one who is truly patient does not wait—they have no expectations. They know that what they seek will come to pass.

Silence and Solitude

In other dimensions of perception, everything is different. Nothing is as it seems—not even within our tangible experiences. Even in what we sense, nothing is truly as it appears. We blend together a cacophony of disparate impressions. To better understand anything, silence must first be established.

I have seen how plants make love. I have witnessed the extension of things intertwining and writhing together. I have lived silence—where a single word, even one letter, could imprison me for an eternity. I have breathed in the solitude of humans amid the chaos of their minds, their tranquility within the turbulence of time. On an empty park bench, I see all the lovers who, lost in each other, press lips in a timeless embrace. The yearning for a kiss, separated by all, cries out in the mirage on a sun-scorched road in the July heat. Even in silence, it screams.

How can I say this? Since the day I became a poet, I have seen things so profound that even the gods are left bewildered by them.

The noise around us is relentless: sound, sound, and more sound. All this clamor exists to drown out the voice of meaning. For if that voice were to reach us, it would all be over.

The silence of a seeker does not arise from a lack of words. It is not something you can will into existence. Silence is born from the immense weight of meaning, under which words crumble and fail. Inevitably, one falls silent. The silence of the seeker is the eruption of meaning in the face of humanity's inability to articulate it.

At a certain point, the seeker begins to perceive without uttering a single word. They understand without being able to express it. They become a mute who ascends to the heavens by night and, by day, struggles futilely to explain their journey. This is the threshold to another truth. Through a single phenomenon, a gesture, or a breath, thousands of volumes of meaning pour into the seeker's mind. They overflow in silence, moving perhaps a hand or nodding a head—alone, in solitude.

"I will whisper hidden secrets into your ear. Just nod and say 'yes,' and say no more."[2]
—Rumi

---

[2] This quote by Rumi suggests a deep, mystical kind of communication, one that goes beyond words and intellectual understanding. When Rumi says, "I will whisper hidden secrets into your ear," he is referring to profound spiritual truths or insights that cannot be fully grasped by the mind. These truths con only be understood on a deeper, intuitive level.

The phrase "Just nod and say 'yes,'" implies that the listener does not need to overthink or question these mysteries. Instead, they should accept and allow these hidden truths to resonate within them, without the need for further explanation or analysis. The message is about surrendering to the experience and trusting in what is being revealed, rather than trying to comprehend everything with the mind.

In ordinary life, there are moments of turning. Sometimes love, sometimes hatred, sometimes an unsolvable problem, or a blow so severe that one doubts they will survive it. It doesn't matter what the turning point is; what matters is that after crossing it, a person is no longer who they were. It is as if they are someone else, capable of erasing their entire history before that moment with a single stroke. They may consider that turning point their new birthday—untethered from the bitter and sweet struggles of that moment.

Seekers experience this as well. From a certain point, a day, an event, or a gesture onward, they can no longer view life, the world, and its unfolding events in the usual way. From one of these points onward, the sacred solitude begins to reveal itself. Something entirely new emerges, to stay forever, resisting every attempt to banish it—though, at times, we may think it has left us.

I do not know if anyone before me has used the term "sacred solitude," but I am certain many have experienced it without naming it. Sacred solitude is the elixir of the awakened heart.

In essence, Rumi is pointing to the importance of inner acceptance and spiritual openness, inviting the listener to embrace wisdom that transcends words. It is a call to trust in the unseen, to feel it deeply without needing to understand it all logically.

It is the kind of intoxication that consumes you without drinking, upending time and space, carrying you to the ascension of meaning.

You fall silent, and yet you crave silence, while simultaneously the tumult of meaning rages within you. Where are the words that could bear the weight of this ambush of meaning, to manifest it? You fall silent, because words are crippled and barren; because the ecstasy within coils and dances in itself, reaching peaks of transcendence; because watching the fiery dance of meaning in silence is intoxicating beyond measure.

Most people reach meanings and concepts through words. But the seeker is immersed in meaning without a single word, sound, or noise. Their words, unlike others, travel in reverse: they arise from meaning and manifest as words. Should they speak, it becomes a masterpiece of eloquence. They compose poetry as if meaning itself is pliable wax in their hands, molding words with masterful artistry.

"I will shatter words, sounds, and speech,
So I may whisper to You beyond all three."
—Rumi

A philosopher (Descartes) once said: "I think, therefore I am." But thinking is the work of the mind. The mind dwells in the past and the future; it has no path to the present moment. In reality, it is when you are not thinking, not caught in thought, and when the mind is quiet, that your true self exists and is present. At all other times, you are absent—enslaved by the mind, which tries to craft meaning through words. But the seeker transforms meaning into words while being entirely present in the moment.

I do not wish to say "mind," or "reason," or "self," or anything else—but whatever exists within a person, with all its noise, strives for one thing alone: its own survival. It wants to describe its own existence, to string together continuity and duration to assert that it is. It wants to say, "I am," and extend that being.

It yearns to express itself and to be acknowledged because its very statements are tools for its survival. If unacknowledged, if there is no exchange of confirmation, its survival is jeopardized; the continuity of its self-descriptive beliefs is threatened. Thus, conversation, speaking, making noise, reasoning, describing—all of it—continues even without external listeners. It becomes an inner dialogue, maintaining its depiction of existence and, consequently, its own place within existence.

This is why, when a person is left alone or remains unacknowledged, they gradually become disheartened, pushed to the margins, and sink into depression. Their continuity is endangered.

The silence I praised earlier is the result of crossing through this solitude: diving into the heart of that obliteration, that annihilation, and emerging on the other side. It is entry into a death that marks the beginning of being truly alive. It is here where one declares:

"Die, die in this love—die!"[3]
—Rumi

There comes a time when a person can no longer muster the strength to describe or seek affirmation. They have made their descriptions but remain unconvinced—even in their dialogue with themselves. No one wishes to hear them anymore, and a sense of futility silences their noise. They reach a point where they accept the futility of further descriptions, the futility of continuation. They concede and accept the absence of persistence, retreating into an internal corner until the last vestiges of their body fade into nothingness.

---

3 In this powerful line, Rumi is encouraging a form of spiritual surrender and transformation. "Die, die in this love—die!" doesn't refer to physical death, but to the idea of letting go of the ego, attachments, and everything that separates a person from pure, unconditional love—particularly divine love.

By "dying," Rumi is urging us to give up our old selves, our pride, our desires, and everything that holds us back from fully experiencing the profound connection to the divine. This "death" is symbolic of a spiritual rebirth, where a person sheds their limited identity and becomes one with the love and truth of the universe.

In essence, Rumi is saying that to truly experience the depth of divine love, one must let go of the self completely, surrendering fully to the experience without resistance or attachment. It is a call to transcend the small, separate self and merge with something greater.

This death, in isolation, in despair, in nihilism—it all stems from the realization that this world, no matter how much you describe it or prolong it, ultimately amounts to nothing. It's a void upon a void, not worth perpetuating.

It is as though you know everything there is, leaving nothing left to uncover—nothing that could ignite the delight of discovery within you, and from that delight, a fresh eagerness to continue.

A single-celled organism, when it divides, is merely making noise—trying desperately to perpetuate itself in utter solitude. It reproduces incessantly, redefining its own existence. In this sense, and by comparison, what deafening chaos is the human being, composed of so many cells! A collection of countless cells, brimming with self-awareness and perception of the surrounding world. And yet, amidst all this, clinging to its insistence: I am! I breathe; therefore, I exist! I endure; therefore, I am!

And how swiftly this insistence collapses into isolation, spiraling toward nonexistence. How effortlessly it renders itself and its surroundings meaningless and void. This extraordinary speed with which we arrive at the brink of futility reveals the emptiness of the ordinary preoccupations of human life in the material world. The meanings here are as shallow as bread and sweets.

This is not to say that the seeker must roam "naked in winter and hungry in summer." Certainly not. These things are no longer their concern. They do not quarrel over them, and their sense of living well is not dependent on such matters. When bread and sweets lose their appeal, the seeker's surroundings grow quieter, disputes diminish, and new meanings find room to emerge. They find their continuity elsewhere and pursue it there. A seeker who returns to worldly matters might engage with life again, but their words, beliefs, quarrels, desires, noise, and even their notions of survival and destruction will no longer resemble what they were before their journey.

Yes, the silence of the seeker does not stem from the absence of words; rather, everything is so perfectly in its place, and the enormity of this perfection renders words unnecessary. Whenever a seeker has spoken, it has been out of ecstasy—a spontaneous outpouring of words, leaping forth to celebrate that vast, indescribable truth. Words come alive, dancing in rhythm, becoming poetry. The greatest wordsmiths of history have always been connected to meaning, regardless of the faith or philosophy they represented.

The essence of meaning itself is inherently silent, wordless, and devoid of sound. Yet, when that silence is broken, the word that emerges is sacred—it is something entirely pure and unprecedented, springing directly from the vessel of meaning. It becomes "The Sacred Word."

"Mary is pregnant without a man—pregnant with Christ,
The silent ones speak with eloquence beyond words."[4]
—Rumi

---

4 In this quote, Rumi is expressing profound spiritual ideas through metaphor.

"Mary is pregnant without a man—pregnant with Christ" refers to the story of the Virgin Mary, who conceived Jesus without the usual physical means of conception. Rumi uses this imagery to symbolize a divine, miraculous form of creation or transformation that happens beyond the physical world or human understanding. In a spiritual sense, being "pregnant with Christ" could mean becoming a vessel for divine love, wisdom, and presence—like Mary, who held Christ within her, we, too, can hold spiritual truths or divine insight within ourselves, even without conventional means.

"The silent ones speak with eloquence beyond words" points to those who have transcended the limitations of ordinary speech. This refers to spiritual individuals who, through deep silence, contemplation, or inner transformation, express profound truths that cannot be captured by language alone. Their communication is not through words, but through presence, actions, or an inner energy that speaks directly to the soul.

Together, Rumi is saying that divine knowledge and wisdom often manifest in ways that go beyond ordinary understanding and words—through silence, inner transformation, and a deeper connection with the divine. It is a reminder that true spiritual insight is not always communicated through speech, but through a more profound, wordless experience.

However you look at it, the creators of literary masterpieces have, in some way, been connected to this essence. At times, these divine manifestations were called revelations in the form of holy books, and at other times, they were simply called poetic inspirations. What is certain is that they have, with words, created something pure and original.

Consider this: the breath of meaning flows like the shepherd's breath through a reed flute. The seeker is that silent reed. All melodies arise from the spiritual breaths of meaning, resonating through the lips of poets. However, not every seeker is a poet, nor is every poet a seeker. The defining trait of the seeker is that they compose in their state of selflessness. Without ecstasy, the conscious ones remain silent and subdued.

Becoming a reed is easy—believe me, it is easy. It requires silence. Many reeds have been carved, but no shepherd has breathed into them. Wind may pass through them, but it is mere air, devoid of the sacred breath of meaning.[5]

---

[5] In this quote, he uses the metaphor of a reed (a hollow pipe or flute) to convey a deeper spiritual message. Becoming a "reed" symbolizes becoming an instrument or vessel for something greater—spiritual insight or divine wisdom. Saying that the physical act of becoming a reed is easy; it is about being open, receptive, and empty, like a reed that has been hollowed out. However, he emphasizes that it is not enough to just be an empty vessel.

Thus, the reed has seven segments, love has seven cities, and the path has seven stages. All of this is metaphor. The reed is a metaphor.

In one night, one can transcend the seven stages and reach seventy—if their measure is so vast that the night becomes their "Night of Destiny." The specific Night of Destiny for each person is hidden among the nights. You cannot search for it deliberately, combing through the nights to find it. You must simply be ready! Let any night that comes, come. Readiness is not a ritual; it is not an act of doing—it is the act of not doing. It is about not being played, not being struck like a reed.

He then says, "It requires silence," meaning that true transformation happens when we silence our inner chatter and distractions, making room for something greater to flow through us. In this stillness, we become capable of receiving divine wisdom or a deeper understanding.

Many reeds may be carved, but without the shepherd's breath—symbolizing divine or spiritual influence—they remain empty, producing nothing more than mere air. Wind passing through them represents life or energy flowing through us, but without the "sacred breath of meaning," it is just superficial or unremarkable.

The deeper message here is that true spiritual transformation requires more than just being open or empty. It requires divine presence or guidance (the "sacred breath") to fill us with purpose, meaning, and a deeper understanding. Without this, our actions and existence may feel empty or lack true direction. The quote encourages us to be receptive to that divine presence, which gives our lives depth and meaning beyond mere existence.

I said becoming a reed is easy, but if you are the reed and you are busy doing something, that "something" is inevitably your being played. The question is: by whom? By the lips of another, or by the lips of the Beloved?

As long as you are doing, as long as you are striving, you do not give the Beloved's lips the chance to play you. As long as you are talking, that pure breath will not be tainted by the breaths of others. And as long as you are seeking, you will not find! It is said: "That which is not found, that is what I long for!"

What cannot be found is not sought—it is longed for.

So, long for it! Searching is a mistake. Any effort to desire or to find it is child's play. Let it desire you. Do not even watch for the moment it arrives! The Beloved is a masterful hunter. Suddenly, you will be caught.

The truth is, the silence of the seeker is not from an inability to speak. Words are tools for meaning. Many silences of seekers are overflowing with meaning, but there is no one to understand them. Sometimes they do not speak because there is no listener, no comprehension—no one who can truly hear and grasp the meaning. Words do not come into being unless there is a listener, for it is the listener who inspires the speaker. Without understanding, the lips remain closed.

"What I speak is to the measure of your understanding,
But I perish in longing for true understanding."
—Rumi

Oh, if only someone would listen and understand! Then, perhaps, the lips would open to speak. It seems this is the great longing of the seekers:

"In this world, if the thirsty seek water,
The water also seeks the thirsty."
—Rumi

Meaning itself thirsts for expression. It is a hidden beauty that cannot bear concealment. How often do we, for countless reasons, fail to open the door to it? It constantly wells up, surges, roars, scratches, and struggles to find a way through:

"If you do not open the door for me, I will climb in through the wall!"[6]
—Rumi

---

[6] To say that meaning itself "thirsts for expression." This is a beautiful metaphor for the idea that truth, beauty, or the essence of life has an innate desire to be shared, expressed, and understood. A force cannot remain hidden forever. He reflects on how often, for various reasons (fear, doubt, societal pressures), we prevent this meaning from flowing freely. Instead of letting it come through, we shut the door.

However, just as the water (truth) seeks the thirsty (the one who is ready to listen), the hidden meaning will find a way to express itself. Humorously says, "If you do not open the door for me, I will climb in through the wall!" This suggests that truth, like an unstoppable force, will eventually find a way to be expressed, even if we try to block it.

On the one hand, meaning is what humanity has lost and seeks. Meaning, awareness, and perfection—three words for the same essence, and countless other unspoken words. Without meaning, a human is an empty shell. Thousands of empty shells do not compare to one full one. This worthiness establishes an eternal struggle in existence—not a battle, but an endless striving on the seeker's path, in continuous connection to meaning.

Without meaning, a person is like a corpse, clawing at anything to find significance. In this futile grasping, they lose pieces of themselves until, one day, even the corpse is gone—nothing left to grasp with, and nothing left to grasp.

This is the story of most people. They spend without earning—bankrupt and meaningless, they spend words without substance, much like parrots do. But even parrots sometimes gain attention, and with this fleeting attention, they extend their existence.

When we use words, we confess something. Confessing reveals us—it is like declaring love to someone. But declaring love is not the same as loving. Loving is action; it leads to behavior, to occurrence. There is always a sequence between desiring, declaring, and occurrence. Most declarations never lead to occurrences. True seeking is occurrence itself. The repetition of occurrence leaves no time for declaration!

Now, do you understand the reason for my silence?

There is a kind of perception that defines and sustains our ordinary human state. Through it, we express everything we perceive and understand.

I have experienced a form of perception that is indescribable. Its speed surpasses explanation, rendering any attempt to articulate what is being perceived impossible. It feels like watching a high-speed performance, where the sheer velocity prevents you from recounting what occurred in the midst of it. In the end, you know you've witnessed something, but there are no words to describe it.

Often, you sense that something has been perceived, yet you can't explain it. You don't even know what to talk about, yet you're aware that you've comprehended many things. This type of perception gradually diminishes the weight of ordinary human understanding, amplifying something else instead. A person begins to feel as though their human form and identity are fading away. The once-busy marketplace of constant conversation disappears, and as conversations dwindle, the desire to be part of gatherings fades too. Silence and solitude become intertwined.

The silence of the seeker does not stem from a lack of words. Meaning is jealous, and in its presence, lips remain sealed. It speaks, while the seeker listens, enraptured. To utter even a single word is to risk losing a thousand others. Meaning is the sole speaker— unceasing, uninterrupted. The seeker is intoxicated, lost in the rhythm of its flow, enraptured in its ecstasy. Occasionally, what they hear bubbles up within them, whispered to their heart, and sometimes even reaches their lips—though only in fragments, often inviting ridicule.

"When drunk and astray come from the tavern's path,
You become the mockery of playful children."
—Rumi

To truly listen, to follow what is being said without losing even a single drop of meaning, the seeker remains silent. Silence becomes a necessity, ensuring that the continuity of understanding is not broken.

A lamp burns brightly, and the seeker gazes at it, intoxicated by its radiance.

In the darkness, a lonely person speaks aloud, whistles, sings—anything to dispel the silence. But all of this is born of fear. If a lamp is lit, the scenario changes, and they fall silent. A lonely person in the dark may quicken their pace, run, shout, make noise. Yet none of this creates light. The faster they run, the more they stumble upon obstacles, injuring themselves, and growing more frightened.

A lonely person in the dark leaps from one relationship to another, from one set of words to another, and from one pitfall to the next. Such a person is like a blindfolded warrior who can be attacked from any direction. The extent of their wounds doesn't matter; what matters is that eventually, the bleeding will bring them to their knees.

A person who does not know themselves or understand their wounds should recognize that shouting will not heal them. In the darkness of the forest, these cries will only attract predators and scare away the delicate deer and singing birds. Their healing lies in silence and the understanding of their own pain. They must first discover the location and nature of their wounds.

I must emphasize that what drives people to seek refuge in others is not loneliness but a lack of self-awareness. Those who know themselves and recognize their own greatness do not seek shelter in others. They may approach others to offer calm but do not rely on others for peace. Solitude is a precious gift that is often squandered in relationships—even in love. Someone who cannot find tranquility within themselves will not find it beside anyone else.

One of the heights seekers reach is a state where they are convinced that they have learned and understood everything, only to realize the profound truth that the world is nothingness upon nothingness.

The emptiness born from such knowing, from such a belief, is like willingly walking into the jaws of death. Yet the truth is, those who walk the path move beyond this nothingness, this land of no-thingness. They do not linger there.

"Beyond the land of nothingness lies a place,
Where man stands alone,
And in that solitude,

The shadow of an elm stretches into eternity."
—Sohrab Sepehri

Our fear of solitude reveals our incompleteness. That which we call perfection is unaffected by either the crowd or loneliness. Perfection, even in its solitude, remains perfect and undiminished. One may run from loneliness, wandering aimlessly, or take deliberate steps in pursuit of perfection. The choice is ours.

Reaching perfection in any endeavor—be it music, knowledge, or any field—does not mean severing ties with others. On the contrary, one may even find their life more crowded, as a master musician, for instance, draws more people to them. But the exclusivity of that perfection guarantees that solitude becomes neither frightening nor barren; rather, it becomes richer than moments spent with others.

One of the most profound joys for a human being is to share what they have with others, to give generously— not as an act of charity, but from a place of magnanimity. Compare the act of sharing one's solitude with sharing one's perfection. In its essence, generosity itself is a form of perfection.

In my view, solitude should not be shared. One should not escape to another to flee from their solitude, for solitude is the sanctuary of love. It is a sacred space where one finds perfection in alignment with their pursuit, whatever it may be. Unfortunately, we often use solitude to dwell on our aloneness, which signals a lack of perfection.

I cannot imagine anything so valuable that I would trade even a moment of my solitude for it. Not that I am sorrowful or depressed—far from it! An immeasurable joy flows within me. Looking back, I see myself lighter with each passing day, my hands free, swaying in the untouched purity of solitude, moving in the invisible rhythm of a divine dance.

I think of the "apple of the world" as trapped in a clay jar, and my hand once caught in that jar, struggling to grasp the apple, unable to free itself. Then I let go of the apple—and in doing so, I became free. And yet, how simple it sounds, how difficult it is to do! Sometimes, I use words and metaphors to describe this bliss, knowing that for many, even half the joy described will suffice. But to truly understand, one must feel the thrill of plucking a fresh apple from abundant branches, free from the jar.

I marvel at those who flee solitude, whose only complaint is loneliness, a yearning for companionship, or the need for constant validation. They are unaware that the beloved resides in solitude. It is there, in that sacred space, where no stranger's feet may tread. In this sense, solitude is where we are with the beloved, united in divine intimacy.

Modern psychology often equates being alone with withdrawal or isolation. And if solitude is devoid of perfection, they are correct. But on the journey toward transcendence and spirituality, there exists a summit where, beneath God's feet, there is solitude. This divine solitude is the epitome of perfection—it knows no sorrow, no depression, no languor. And toward that summit, we are all traveling, drawn toward a unique sun that rises behind a solitary mountain.

Even if one, overwhelmed by loneliness, seeks a partner among the crowd and finally finds their match, they inevitably devote themselves entirely to that companion. From the perspective of others, it appears they have disconnected from the world;

While surrounded by people, one may find the greatest solitude—taking immense pleasure in this separation from the crowd. Such a person retreats not out of fear or disdain but because they have discovered within themselves a grandeur that rivals, if not surpasses, the entire external world.

This inner companion, linked to the individual moment by moment, creates a state where the two feel as though they are one. It fosters a belief in the greatness within until one proclaims, "I am the Truth" (Ana al-Haqq). The self merges with the divine self, exclaiming, "Subhāni, mā a'zam shāni!" (Glory to me, how great is my being!)— declaring that they and the divine are inseparable. "Who am I? Layla. And who is Layla? Me."[7]

---

[7] The passage explores the idea of solitude in a deeper, spiritual context. While modern psychology might see being alone as a form of withdrawal or loneliness, the text suggests another kind of solitude, which is divine and perfect. This kind of solitude is not about sadness or isolation, but rather about the state of spiritual fulfillment and closeness to the sacred. It is the idea that true transcendence comes when a person

The belief that the seeker withdraws to pursue isolation is a complete misunderstanding. Similarly, the notion that retreating into seclusion will smooth the path of spiritual journeying is a grave error. True journeying is a unification with everything, at least from the seeker's perspective. As they immerse themselves in the crowd, they find themselves feeling more alien. The more they

---

reaches a place where they are at peace with themselves and God.

The passage also describes how someone might seem to withdraw from the world, even when surrounded by others, because they have found a deep sense of connection and inner peace that makes external companionship less necessary. They feel a profound connection to their inner self, linked to the divine, to such an extent that they might declare, "I am the Truth," suggesting unity with God. The famous mystical saying "Ana al-Haqq" (I am the Truth) refers to a spiritual state where the person feels that their identity and the divine are one.

The reference to "Layla" at the end likely alludes to a famous Sufi story of the lovers Layla and Majnun, where Layla symbolizes the soul's longing for union with the divine. The phrase "Who am I? Layla. And who is Layla? Me" represents the merging of the individual self with the divine.

This passage draws from Sufi mysticism, particularly from the works and teachings of mystics like Ibn Arabi and Rumi, who often spoke of the soul's journey toward union with the divine. The concept of "I am the Truth" (Ana al-Haqq) is famously attributed to the Sufi mystic al-Hallaj, who proclaimed his oneness with God before facing persecution for such a claim.

interact, the more distant they feel until, finally, they ask, "What have I to do with this gathering?" They understand everything about those around them, yet no one truly understands them.

Thus, their solitude resembles the solitude of a candle in darkness: casting light on everything around it while receiving no illumination in return. From the outside, they appear engaged in their task, quiet and detached, without any interaction. After all, what dialogue can fire have with its surroundings, other than to consume them? The seeker burns through everything, reducing it to ash. Hence, people of meaning seem isolated and unreachable, much like the sun, which, though distant, radiates warmth and remains deeply connected to the world.

These words are not mere descriptions but reflections on the summit of spiritual realization, where the sovereign of understanding and meaning sits alone. The closer one approaches this pinnacle, the more profound their solitude becomes. Such is the nature of love: it is demanding, exclusive, separating you from others and drawing you entirely into itself. Yet, since there is no true separation, you see everything as part of yourself.

I share this so that you may understand: whenever your conversation—or even your silence—with others elevates you beyond solitude, awakening a feeling as though you no longer share a common language, know that this is a sign. It signals that this group is not yours, and you must return to the realm of your heart.

Strengthen yourself for the wandering desert, but do not take refuge in the city of fleeting comforts.

Solitude is a profound concept. True solitude belongs to the one who has purified themselves from all things and holds nothing within but meaning. The physical body cannot comprehend or bear the enormity of such spiritual grandeur. It begins to twist, contort, and sway, seizing upon anything it can to tether itself—spinning, spiraling, and dancing.

The dance in the seeker's body emerges from this source—a state of intoxicated movement. Their poetry is the dance of words. Their generosity is the dance of possessions. Their love is the dance of pride. Sometimes, I imagine meaning as a woman, dancing—dancing entirely alone. Graceful, poised, she twirls within herself, swaying and stirring. Her every movement sets off a storm of energy.

The solitude and detachment of individuals are not determined by the number of people surrounding them. In my view, being lonely in a crowd reflects a deeper solitude. Physical isolation, on its own, creates separation, but it lacks the richness of solitude found in the midst of others.

In the end, some renounce the world to avoid everything, while others immerse themselves in it, chasing after everything. But a third group—those who are present in the moment—stand apart. Whether witnessing a king reigning over his realm or a beggar wandering the streets, they see goodness in the occurrence itself and remain the silent witnesses of that goodness, even when it appears otherwise to the eyes of the world.

One must not overlook the significant distinction that while a spiritual individual is devoid of the feeling of loneliness, they can often be overwhelmed by a profound sense of vulnerability. This vulnerability is the most fundamental realization that appears at the threshold of the spiritual journey—a harbinger of the opening of perception beyond the ordinary world.

For me personally, this feeling was immense and frightening. I didn't understand its cause; it lay beyond the grasp of my daily comprehension. Even in the mundane life of an ordinary person, there are moments when one feels exposed and defenseless, but this spiritual vulnerability cannot be compared to that. The seeker's vulnerability stems from an entirely different source. Suddenly, in the midst of understanding oneself, you see everything and everyone separate from you, and you find yourself utterly alone in the vastness of existence.

It was only later that I came to understand this sensation as a powerful pull from the realm of meaning—an all-encompassing force drawing us in. Our awareness of this, when set against the overwhelming inertia of being one with meaning, gives rise to this feeling of defenselessness. It is akin to a person who watches as a flood carries away everything and everyone they know.

To me, this powerful pull obstructs the ability to fully know oneself. It is the source of all the difficulty in the spiritual path. The seeker, in attempting to comprehend their own essence, seems to shake the very foundation of existence, only to confront a profound truth: in the vast solitude of their being, they are deeply vulnerable.

The foundation of worship-based beliefs is built upon this very feeling. Whether it involves the worship of stone idols, celestial bodies, or the illusions of theistic gods, it all arises from the seeker's sense of spiritual vulnerability. Following this monumental error, humans transfer the immense force of this pull to a god or idol, making it powerful and seeking refuge in its presence.

We observe that the more followers a god has, the more powerful and capable it appears. This power arises from multiplying the number of devotees by the inertia of their collective vulnerability. But I did not take this path. I did not use this tremendous force to empower an imagined god.

Instead, I surrendered myself to it. I allowed myself to remain afloat in the ecstasy of perceiving my separateness, while simultaneously being guided by it— connected to meaning, wherever it chose to take me. The result of this experience was that despite the magnitude of my vulnerability, I found myself held by a force that was strong and steadfast yet utterly familiar, akin to me.

I was not a servant to it; its power was my own. And this power was not expended for dominion or control but for the purpose of remaining peacefully connected to all things, to all beings, and to the entirety of existence.

This way, no god is born, no power is amassed, and no wars are waged in the name of one god's strength over another or one interpretation of god against another. This is a connection to the infinite—free of conflict, free of division.

Rationality in the Spiritual Path

Carl Gustav Jung, in his exploration of the psychological problems of modern humans in a book of the same name, writes:

"There are aspects of nature within us that seem hidden from our view, and we have taken refuge behind the walls of reason to shield ourselves from them. Analytical psychology, by extracting the imaginative images of the unconscious from the oblivion into which rationality has cast them, seeks to penetrate this wall. These images lie beyond the wall and to those who break through these walls; there is a profound sense of magnificence. Yet, the walls of rationality separate us from the eternal essence of nature, confining us to an era where intellect reigns supreme and shackles us within the narrow confines of time—a space suspended between birth and death. It is within this confinement that the feelings of emptiness and futility arise, obstructing us from living with the seriousness life demands and ultimately preventing us from triumphing over life itself. "

I selected these reflections from Jung because of the profound wisdom with which he speaks of the human psyche. For this, I hold him in great respect. However, his acknowledgment of rationality as a logical man holds a different meaning for me, for my heart-driven beliefs seldom seek the arithmetic of logic in perception.

Rationality is the art of distinguishing between good and bad, choosing from among the options. It is the act of calculating which choice is better and selecting it. This means being in the midst of a battle where victory depends on making the right choices. Yet, if one errs in their choice, defeat is inevitable, and the loser of that game becomes the defeated in that battle.

This flawed belief forms the foundation of the deadlock in which modern humanity is trapped. I too once embraced rationality, but rationality is akin to saying that a person must remain dependent on their mother's milk for life. Milk is the nourishment of infancy—a sustenance needed to stand on one's feet, to survive until reaching a stage of growth where one can consume solid food. Beyond that, it is no longer beneficial and may even cause harm.

Intellect is for taking the first steps. Beyond a certain point, intellect no longer suffices; cunning and calculation become irrelevant. The statement "I want to live well" is the most logical and reasonable aspiration of a balanced and rational person. However, in my view, even when accompanied by genuine effort and determination to transform into action, this aspiration marks the beginning of living poorly—an initiation into repeated failures and frustrations along life's path.

Declaring "I want" is an act of calculation, division, and logic—a decision made with certainty. It is like choosing to spend the remainder of life in infancy, a child fixated on a singular choice. Human judgment, however, does not stop at the external world. One judges everything, even their own welfare, based on their assessment.

Judgment is valid only when all dimensions of a matter are understood. When parts of the issue remain hidden, how can one judge, or have confidence in their judgment? Humanity relies solely on its assumptions, choosing what seems the best option based on judgment. Each time this judgment fails, hope shifts to the next decision. The ultimate judgment occurs at the moment of death—if time permits.

It is then that victories and defeats are tallied, and the sum of life is evaluated. Alas, humanity often finds itself the loser, with the first accurate judgment arriving in the final moments. In that instant, one regrets what they themselves squandered. To say, "I want to live well," is akin to saying, "I want to win this chess game." Victory in chess cannot exist without defeat. If one does not win in chess, the alternative is to lose.

The concept of winning and losing, deeply ingrained in our rational decision-making, becomes the greatest obstacle to what is called "living well." The issue arises from the belief that life is a battle—that goals must be defined, pursued, and fought for relentlessly.

Life is not a battle; it is a complex game—a game within games, filled with interconnected and recurring branches and layers. We are neither white pieces fighting black nor black pieces against white. This belief is profoundly mistaken. Life may indeed appear as a chessboard, with each person's life a battlefield of black and white pieces moving across black and white squares. These pieces carry infinite possibilities in their moves yet remain interlinked.

It does not matter whether white or black wins in a single game; what matters is that the chessboard provides the stage for these pieces to move in harmony. Every game has a beginning and an end, and the board remains impartial yet central to the game. Without it, the game cannot occur. However, each time we play, we perceive ourselves as either white or black. And the perpetual belief in being a loser blinds us to the truth: we are the synthesis of both colors, untouched by any victory or defeat.

The absence of awakened spiritual thought connected to meaning is a profound loss. Without it, thought is inevitably shaped by external influences. Spiritual perception is like a fluid flow; any material imposition obstructs it, nullifies it, or creates false illusions. The elevation of spiritual perception occurs in a state of semi-consciousness, a kind of intoxication, a perceptual slip.

One might remain entirely unaware of this elevation in their usual state of consciousness, perhaps even for a lifetime. Yet meaning continues its ceaseless flow, slipping and gliding forward without interruption.

Our desires are generally trivial, insignificant, and fleeting. Achieving them brings us joy, and to attain them, we compete, struggle, and sometimes fight fiercely with others. Often, rejecting and surpassing others becomes a prerequisite for fulfilling these desires. This structure mercilessly designs the world in such a way that the survival of one depends on the destruction of another.

In contrast, great desires are achieved through camaraderie, convergence, and reconciliation, where rivals transform into friends. It does not matter how significant or minor these desires seem to us; what matters is which category they fall into based on the above definition. This criterion is clear and precise.

Sharing wealth diminishes its quantity and fosters competition. However, sharing pure music expands its presence. A person finds joy in sharing it with another, and the fact that others derive equal pleasure creates empathy and amplifies joy.

In my view, humanity is a strange being. It has the ability to imagine, to create dreams, and then to live within the atmosphere of those dreams, taking them seriously to the point of fighting for them, killing for them, being killed for them, making the world bitter or sweet because of them. In the end, though, without those dreams, one could imagine different ones and create an entirely different world. Perhaps these differences in dreams have caused many misunderstandings and moments of mutual understanding. Yet even without them, life would continue to flow.

I believe humans are the only creatures that set traps and then fall into their own traps. They imagine, dream, and believe that everything is progressing well, only to suddenly realize there's no path forward. The more traps they create, the greater their chances of being ensnared.

This relentless pursuit of acquisition is a gradual death along the spiritual path—a process of losing everything worldly that is valuable. Although this task is challenging, it is achievable. At a stage where the seeker separates from everything, they sense a unique ability within themselves—a feeling that everything in the world is aligning for them. They desire nothing, yet whatever occurs seems to miraculously fall into place in harmony with them.

This is one of the most perilous passages along the path. The pride born from this realization can destroy nearly everything, consuming the seeker's life entirely. It leads to ruin after ruin and years of stagnation. Pride will be explored in greater detail in a separate chapter.

Reflections on the Realm of Meaning

I am connected to an infinite expanse of something indescribable.
It cannot be put into words, yet I know it exists. I see it with a clarity that remains hidden from others. The hardest part is that silence, in its very essence, amasses a weight that feels as though it might shatter me from within tearing me apart! Speaking of love is difficult, but silence, perhaps, is even harder.

I grapple with concepts and connections that the mind cannot merely recall, let alone explain. Yet, I grasp them! Even describing this state is challenging. Imagine a flash of lightning in the sky: one understands that something has occurred, but its speed may prevent one from capturing its shape, direction, or magnitude. Something is understood, yet there are no tools adequate to measure it.

The truth is, our eyes have grown accustomed to darkness, and light becomes a burden to them. The illumination of insight is unwelcome to eyes accustomed to the dark; it even obstructs their vision. We turn away, close our eyes, give in to fear, and retreat—remaining in the confined and darkened hole of our limited perception.

Meaning desires to manifest—not in the sense of becoming visible, for it is always in a state of manifestation, both in what is apparent to us and what is not. Instead, it seeks to be perceived. I believe that this very desire for perception gives rise to its manifestations. These occurrences, however, are often understood only through themselves and nothing else.

Meaning gathers within itself. In its essence, it is singular and whole, but outwardly, it is dispersed like clouds, scattered, and hence rarely evident. One must seize it in an instant of imagination and touch it fleetingly, for if not, it vanishes entirely. We attempt to be clever: we first let go of being, and then, in a moment and in an instant, everything is turned upside down. No one knows what I am saying. I speak to ensure it remains.

This property of meaning gives rise to the deepest longing among seekers. The seeker, connected to meaning, possesses an inherent yearning to be understood. This desire keeps the channel of meaning open within the seeker. The irony lies in the fact that what must be understood—what the seeker yearns to let pass through them—remains incomprehensible to others. This is a profound sorrow, representing a blockage in the flow of meaning and halting further progress.

The eloquence of the seeker in prose and poetry stems from their struggle to convey and reopen this passageway. Often, this endeavor remains unfulfilled within the short span of a human life. If even one person, just one, grasps the meaning expressed and revealed by another at the moment of its manifestation, it is an invaluable treasure.

"The measure of a companion who breathes in harmony,

no one knows like me."
—Saadi[8]

Is it possible to train someone and transfer to them the perception of meaning gained through insight? Meaning can penetrate anything—this is its inherent property—and it can dwell in all things. However, perceiving it requires an internal quality, which comes with varying levels and unique challenges. These challenges can be so profound that transferring meaning to an object may seem easier than to another human being who ostensibly seeks it.

Finding the right individual for this process is a significant risk. Sometimes, the right person may emerge, equipped with suitable qualities, but even then, one cannot impose it upon them. In truth, an internal acceptance process within the individual is required.

At the next stage, such a person, placed in the appropriate environment, may cry out, lose consciousness, go mad, or even lose their life upon the slightest connection to the perception of meaning. It is an arduous, exhausting, and time-consuming process.

---

8 Saadi (1210–1291/1292): Saadi Shirazi was a renowned Persian poet and prose writer of the medieval period, celebrated for his eloquence, wisdom, and humanistic values. His most famous works, *Gulistan* (The Rose Garden) and *Bustan* (The Orchard), combine moral guidance with storytelling and poetry, offering insights into ethics, society, and spirituality. Saadi's universal messages of tolerance, justice, and compassion have made him a timeless figure in Persian literature and beyond.

When I say time-consuming, it is not a universal rule. For some, a single gesture might result in miraculous new perceptions. To explain, consider a person bound firmly to a solid pillar. This connection to the pillar defines all their material perceptions. The rope binding them is strong and unbreakable, and the pillar itself is immovable. Freedom from this pillar is no simple task. Yet occasionally, for one reason or another, the pillar is uprooted!

A strong strike—whether by chance, fate, or fortune—might dislodge or even shatter this pillar. Once such an event occurs, a person's perceptions are transformed. The most pressing question then is: what happens in such a state? Imagine a container of water placed in a vast ocean. The water within the container belongs to the same ocean, yet it is segregated. When the event occurs, at the very least, the container is emptied and refilled. For the identity previously contained within, this is an utterly astonishing experience. The other possibility is for the container to be entirely submerged in the ocean!

Submersion causes that distinct identity to dissolve, become lost, and irretrievable, while simultaneously merging with greatness and experiencing a form of eternal existence in a new identity. In my view, this is not the path of the seeker. Every human being ultimately dissolves into this ocean. I sought to preserve that distinct identity while simultaneously merging with that infinite greatness—to experience eternity while maintaining self-awareness and individuality.

This means that all human actions originate from meaning itself, with the least friction between the unspoken essence and our defined perceptual identity. I perceive forces that have shaped this separation. Yet, in truth, there is no separation. What exists, I cannot name or differentiate. One thing is clear: the smallest part—insignificant to the point of neglect—while still entirely part of the larger whole, can perceive itself and extend this understanding. I call such extension immortality, though it remains unclear how far this can truly extend.

Although I have grasped a few subtle aspects of meaning, my knowledge is nearly nothing. When I explain these insights, I am not a witness observing from a distance, detached from the matter. Instead, I am part of this phenomenon, experiencing a separate perception.

I have perceived certain sounds, waves, and states, which I will explain further in this section. However, before delving into those, it is essential to discuss the subject of hearing and understanding these sounds, waves, and states:

I am a listener. Listening is the best way to perceive the universe. The essence and continuity of this perception rely on dialogue. Listening is not about hearing with the ears because no ear is capable of such listening, and it should not be mistaken with the conventional meaning of the word. Listening is the ability to reinterpret everything—all that constitutes you in an instant and whose existence enables your being. Listening is an unmediated understanding, a comprehension without sensation. Listening is akin to recalling a dream you once had. It is like remembering a line from a book, the most important line from a forgotten book. Listening is rereading a book line by line from a hidden memory. It is like three-dimensional images on paper that slowly emerge when you cross your eyes, sparking joy upon their revelation.

Listening is a continuous repetition that builds a fresh understanding. It is something absent from this world yet connected to it. Listening is the bridge to seeing the unseen. It is the sensation of the insensible. Listening is a form of disregard for what is already known; it is unhearing the known, believing in the unseen, in what defies logic, in a language you cannot comprehend yet understand. Listening is like the subtle signals exchanged in the gaze of lovers—it is knowing without words.

The "heard" has a dimension, if it can be called that. Not everyone can endure every dimension. The volume of what is heard can easily separate the soul from the body. It can make the listener unconscious or lull them into a sleep that drains their energy. Listening stems from breath, from a wave—a pervasive wave that encompasses everything in visible existence. Listening does not originate from sound. There is no sound to listen to. While there is sound in existence, it is not related to this kind of listening.

I have experienced three types of sounds[9], none of which are connected to this form of listening:

A sound resembling "buzzzzz," spinning without direction and fleeting, akin to the whistling of a bullet. This buzzing sound has oscillations, as though approaching and receding from the listener, with a final whistle and a renewed oscillation.

A sound like a stormy suction, or as if water is being forcefully drawn into a cavity. It appears rotational, though no actual rotation occurs. If you round your lips and inhale sharply, you might replicate this sound, though it lacks the awe and intensity of the original. I have often heard this sound at the onset of changes in perception, and it ceases the moment the perception changes. Upon returning to previous perceptions, this sound does not recur.

Another sound is rhythmic pounding with regular intervals. Imagine bowing your head and then straightening your neck—a pounding occurs. This rhythm is sometimes fast, sometimes slower, but always consistent. The sound becomes faster as one approaches dark boundaries and diminishes upon moving away from them, ultimately fading. Therefore, the rhythm of this pounding sound signifies proximity to dark boundaries. When this pounding increases, the

---

9 This concept is often linked to intuition, inner knowing, or even a spiritual or subconscious recognition of truth. It's the kind of "hearing" or "understanding" that goes beyond the physical senses—like when you deeply "feel" the essence of something or grasp a meaning that isn't explicitly stated.

"buzzzzz" sound ceases. At times, I have heard a combination of these two sounds.

These experiences of listening are not through the ears, and someone sitting beside you would hear nothing. However, these three sounds differ from the intended meaning of pure listening, as that listening occurs in absolute silence. It is a kind of listening to silence, an understanding of silence.

It should be noted that this perception and its outcomes are not permanent; they dissipate rapidly in ordinary states. This listening is neither revelation nor inspiration. It may result from revelation seated in one's being, but in itself, it can only recall parts of that revelation. It is not inspiration, nor is it illusion, though it can initially be tainted with illusions. When one becomes purified by imagination and dwells in the realm of imagination, the path of illusions to this listening is closed. By revelation here, I refer to the meaning conceived in religious beliefs.

The Dark Realm

Within the dark realm lies an infinite expanse, akin to an ocean within which all that is not dark is submerged. I neither know its depths nor its boundaries, neither its extent nor its end, nor have I dared to drift within it. This limitless domain is a form of nonexistence—a kind of void. I cannot comprehend what it truly is. Everything that is observable within our existence is submerged within it, and it is conceivable that countless realms akin to what we perceive as existence are also engulfed within its depths.

The Illuminated Realm

Within this dark realm exists an illuminated realm, and all that is observable within our existence resides in this domain. The essence of this realm is wave-like. Initially, I believed there were two waves: one spreading outward, pushing and radiating, and the other pulling inward, magnetic and consuming. Later, I realized that it is, in fact, a single wave—emanating outward on one side and being drawn back inward on the other, creating a circular motion. This wave displays the appearance of two waves, and from each, two additional waves emerge. In total, there are four primary waves, and from each primary wave, six smaller waves radiate, forming a total of twenty-eight waves that shape and influence our observable existence.

The primary wave radiates within the dark realm, and in reality, it constitutes the vast majority of the illuminated realm, which cannot be described. It is beyond my ability to explain and could only be comprehended by one observing it from within the dark realm—a feat that is impossible. I recognize the dark realm by the magnitude of this wave, as it defines the boundaries of the illuminated realm. Within the illuminated realm and the domain of this wave, there are spaces filled with the dark realm. These spaces fluctuate in size, sometimes shrinking and sometimes expanding, but their overall trend is toward contraction. The reason for this is time.

Time exists in the illuminated realm but is meaningless in the dark realm. Time only pushes against the boundaries of the dark realm. Approaching the edges of the dark realm renders everything suspended; there is no perception of time or space. Near these boundaries, time becomes faintly perceptible, a pure intoxication that carries a slight sense of passing time and nothing more. Nothing can rescue a seeker from this state or prevent their dissolution into non-being except for the ordinary five senses, which act as handles for returning.

I have never heard, in my pure listening experiences, anyone recount what occurs within the dark realm. I have reached its edges, and what I know is this: no perception, in the usual sense, exists for me there. My secondary perception, however, felt drawn toward that realm, and had it not been for the usual level of awareness, I would have undoubtedly dissolved into its darkness.

The sound of rhythmic pounding emanating from the dark realm is the only thing that can be observed from it. I know nothing about the source of this sound. Its regularity offers no guarantee that an orderly source is producing it. Perhaps the emergence of the illuminated realm holds a clue for those who come after us.

The entire existence of the illuminated realm resembles a spark or the vibration of lightning in the sky—no more. Everything that is observable and perceptible within human existence amounts to a single fleeting moment in comparison to the dark realm. It has occurred, ended, and the spark has subsided.

Is the sound of the pounding a result of the emergence of other worlds? I do not know. Is it the sound of the conclusion of other worlds? I do not know. Never has it been possible to approach the dark realm and, within its trance, return to ordinary perception with the same awareness. The return has always been to natural awareness.

Thus, our understanding of time—regardless of how swiftly or slowly it flows in either state, or its comparison to the absence of time in the dark realm— indicates that our perceived time moves incomprehensibly faster relative to the dark realm. From the perspective of the dark realm, the illuminated realm is merely a concluded event.

In truth, we live within a temporal coordinate system that has already reached its end, like a flash of lightning in the sky. Now, we are experiencing the serene afterglow of that lightning, and our destined path is already determined.

I know nothing more of the dark realm, nor will I attempt to describe it further. Perhaps in the course of this exploration, I may touch upon it again, depending on the context. But I do not know what the dark realm truly is. Is it nothingness? Perhaps not. Are there other worlds within it? I do not know. How was it created? I do not know. Is it a creation itself? I cannot say.

The dark realm has no coordinates to define it, no point where one could declare that the spark of the illuminated realm originated. Yet, at the moment of its occurrence, time began, and the radius of its spread formed dimensions.

The knowledge that modern physics has gathered thus far—whether right or wrong—is tied to what lies beyond this point. What I will explain is my understanding, expressed in my own language:

The dark realm, the smoke, the illumination, along with the dark voids, the smoke again, and the dark realm— this is the entire sequence of events, which from our temporal perspective takes billions of years.

The initial smoke signifies the birth of our existence, while the illumination represents the spread of consciousness and awareness within it. The secondary smoke indicates the withdrawal of consciousness, ultimately returning to the dark realm.

What I mean by consciousness is not human understanding but rather the laws that can expand, change, or even be defied across the universe. From this perspective, gravity is consciousness, repulsion is consciousness, magnetism is consciousness. The relationships between atoms, genes, and molecules are manifestations of consciousness. What resides in the nucleus of an atom is consciousness, as is the force that holds celestial bodies in their orbits. This consciousness emerges, shapes everything in its path, and then dissipates.

When this consciousness arises, it harmonizes all it encounters with itself. Whatever fails to align with it is transformed. Through this process, consciousness expands and evolves until it reaches its final point, where it ceases.

I am neither a philosopher nor a scientist, and the task of expanding these statements falls to those who are equipped with the knowledge and passion to explore such matters—provided they are not ridiculed, as with the early idea of the Earth being round.

This awareness, this spreading light in the form of the illuminated realm, has created galaxies, celestial bodies, and everything within them. But from what? From the smoke before the flash of lightning. And how does it end? The lightning subsides, the smoke returns, and all is complete. Will there be another? Is there a repetition of this process? I do not know.

Here on Earth, this consciousness has completed itself and continues its progression. We exist here and now, in this place and moment, as a result of it. The accumulation of this consciousness led to the formation of atoms, elements, minerals, plants, and animals. A more profound aggregation of this consciousness brought forth life itself—culminating in humans.

In humans, the accumulation of this consciousness transcended mere life; it gave rise to the word. The word was heard, and thus, I am now a listener—one who listens, born from the unique convergence of this spark of awareness within the smoke. A spark that brought order and law to everything.

It is clear, then, that behind all that you perceive and experience through your senses, there is smoke imbued with governing laws. This smoke, containing such laws, exists in the dark realm alongside the flashes of consciousness that manifest as illumination.

The human form is the result of countless laws born from the accumulation of consciousness. This consciousness manifests as light, as radiance that can be perceived. The extent of this radiance reflects the depth of our awareness. Our perception is interconnected, bound together in such a way that my understanding may arise from seeing, hearing, touching, smelling, or tasting. These senses are distinct yet complementary; they are one in their essence.

What this perception comprehends is directly proportional to the level of my consciousness. If I encounter something beyond my awareness, this perception becomes distorted. And what happens when my perception is distorted? My understanding falters, and I face challenges in grasping the nature of what I encounter.

Pride

The path of meaning demands courage, not pride. To be proud is not the same as to be brave; one can be cowardly and yet full of pride. Personal importance fuels pride. The pride born of personal importance makes us cowards, yet it falsely grants us the illusion of bravery. This kind of pride repels the blessings that the universe bestows upon us—a devastating loss, almost impossible to recover from.

The absence of personal importance should not be confused with passivity or submission to others. Self-respect and personal importance are two entirely different concepts. A seeker possesses self-respect but is free from personal importance and pride. They are not weak or a pawn to be manipulated by others.

The obsessive defense of personal pride, which ultimately destroys everything we hold dear, is less an ethical or social behavior and more a biological mechanism for survival. In truth, our subconscious fights to preserve our human identity—a fragile identity that is under the control of ruthless usurpers. This battle is but a subtle effort to guard the camp of our permanent captivity.

Within us sits a merciless usurper, seeking to claim everything for itself. To do so, it must assert its primacy in every possible way. It dictates our sense of importance, convincing us that we are more significant than anything else. Once we accept this illusion, our desires become our ultimate goals. This selfishness forms the strongest and most unyielding cage, trapping us within ourselves. That usurper drains the very essence of our awareness in this manner.

All teachings in various schools of thought about selflessness are, in truth, exercises to overcome this usurper. Sacrifice, altruism, benevolence, and countless other virtues exist solely to free us from this suffocating cage.

Human beings, proud of a false identity, lost in a virtual existence, delight in fleeting pleasures that ultimately leave them hollow. They spin in endless circles until death finds them. Is this a tragedy? No. But it is an undeniable reality.

You ask me, what is the greatest obstacle? I have often said: pride and selfishness! In essence, it is self-absorption, followed by self-attack, and ultimately self-harm. Like the tale of the lion that saw its reflection in the well, attacked itself, and fell in.

"You strike yourself, oh simple man,
Like the lion[10] that struck at itself!" (Rumi)

---

10 The story of the lion in this context is derived from a parable used by Rumi in his works. It illustrates the dangers of pride, self-deception, and lack of self-awareness.

In the tale, a lion comes across a well and, upon looking into it, sees its own reflection in the water. Mistaking the reflection for another lion, it perceives it as a threat or rival. Driven by pride and the need to defend its territory, the lion attacks the

Whatever you see in others is but a reflection in that well. You might think you see yourself as larger, greater, or even more deserving. It is not so. The true reality of you is precisely what you see around you. This world is a palace of mirrors. Wherever weakness resides, pride appears. Perhaps its only virtue lies in this: pride reveals our weaknesses better than anything else.

On the spiritual path, restraint and inner strength replace pride. In the face of the unknown, pride is utterly useless. In fact, its presence in moments where one confronts the vastness of meaning and finds oneself small and powerless can cause complete collapse. In such moments, even a speck of pride can lead one to feel utterly worthless. This sense of worthlessness prompts one to step aside, to remove oneself from the path of what lies ahead. Such self-preservation is, in truth, the protection of ego and pride, rooted deeply in the instinct for survival.

---

reflection by leaping into the well. Tragically, it drowns as a result of this act.

This story serves as an allegory for human behavior. The lion's attack on its reflection symbolizes how people, blinded by pride or ego, can misinterpret situations or their own nature. In doing so, they harm themselves, much like the lion. The "self-attack" represents self-destructive tendencies born from misunderstanding and self-absorption. Rumi's verse reminds us of this flaw, urging us to let go of pride and illusions to avoid self-inflicted harm.

"Die, die to this self, sever your ties,
For this self is a chain, and you are its captive." (Rumi)

The path of Sufism is a journey of inner strength, yet if
this strength is not tempered by self-restraint, the power
derived from this strength can give rise to a new form of
pride—one far more challenging to overcome than the
initial pride. This time, the pride emerges from a sense of
power that perceives no obstacle before it, leading one
onto a path that could consume the seeker's entire life,
trapping them in its grip.

Flawless Authority

Humans are physically weak creatures, yet in the realm of meaning, when focused on something particular, they possess astounding power. There are moments when no strength exists to act, and nothing happens. Then there are times when the ability to do anything is present, yet nothing worthy of action exists, and still, nothing happens. Are these two the same? No, they are not.

"What can a fragile vessel do in the torrent of annihilation?
When the flood rises, no water remains in the jug."

I have seen other beings who, when a human gathers themselves in meaning, circle them like moths around a flame, yearning for the radiance of this gathered meaning in one place, striving to take their share. The gathering of a human in meaning resembles earthly love when, detached from all else, you see only one and dissolve entirely into it. Some, at their height, are consumed by a lofty love, while others, in a descent, are enamored by a mere visage. The difference between the two is vast.

To act flawlessly, one requires authority, and authority arises from acting flawlessly. This cycle is the only means of survival on the treacherous path of Sufism. Authority and its effects behave like a wild, powerful horse. It can be a sturdy, reliable steed if tamed, yet it can also throw you to the ground and take your life.

The horse of authority cannot be approached, bridled, and subdued like a docile animal. The truth is, one day,

On our path

you suddenly find yourself riding its back, while it bucks and thrashes! At that moment, something within you must be ready—something decisive in whether you remain seated or are thrown to the ground with your bones shattered.

An empowered individual is not like a king riding a horse of pride. More often, they are an unassuming seeker who desires nothing, while all desires bow before them. The greatest achievement on the path is authority—an authority that understands solutions emerge from intentional will, not from complaints or lamentations. The seeker comes to realize that the level of authority is a potent lever in achieving objectives, and the greater the authority, the shorter the time to attain results.

It matters not whether the obstacle before the seeker is a frail wall of straw or a massive mountain range; they will pass beyond it.

"I am not one to bow to the whims of the cruel heavens. If fate opposes me, I will overturn the celestial sphere." – Hafez[11]

---

[11] Hafez (1315–1390), one of Iran's most celebrated poets, is renowned for his profound and lyrical ghazals that explore themes of love, spirituality, and the mysteries of existence. His divan (collection of poems) reflects a deep understanding of Sufism, blending mysticism with a sharp critique of hypocrisy. Hafez's poetry continues to hold a revered place in Persian culture, often used for divination and inspiration, and his works have been widely translated, resonating with readers across the world.

66

Natural obstacles in life do not evoke hatred within us. We never consider taking revenge on a flood; we merely step aside to preserve ourselves. Step aside from whatever you dislike! Calming it is not your task; like a flood, it will eventually find its stillness elsewhere.

Your task is to learn how to preserve yourself. This preservation is not selfish—it is self-restraint. Each time you hold yourself back from anger, pride, lust, or hatred, your soul gains greater authority until no flood can uproot it.

Preserving Personal Authority

Preserving personal authority is neither selfishness nor pride. Sometimes, all you need to do is lower your head and move forward—in a state of utmost humility. The soul of existence will undoubtedly recognize and reward this humility of yours.

Your role is not to guide others. Their education or transformation is not your responsibility. Nothing diminishes the authority of a seeker more than the failure of others to comprehend meanings. Step aside from their path as well! Those who are destined for the journey will cross your path again, at higher levels of authority—when they themselves have found their way to meaning—without wasting your spiritual authority.

Do not resist those who, in any way, drain your energy. Neither seek closeness to them nor distance yourself from them. Simply acknowledge whatever they say, desire, or do—without any additional action or deliberate reaction. They will suffer more from this lack of confrontation than you can imagine, and eventually, they will part ways with you on their own. The path of the seeker is a flight—at its peak, and always solitary.

Flawless behavior is not the product of thinking or planning; it is born of inner authority. This authority can turn a faint chance into a guaranteed opportunity. Actions stemming from authority cannot be planned, taught, or learned. They rely entirely on their own essence. After they occur, one realizes that something has been accomplished, and in the best possible way—without any prior plan.

Acts of authority are flawless and impose themselves on everything—on all that seeks meaning! In truth, we know that meaning seeks nothing and is wholly an act of becoming—manifesting in infinite and novel forms. Many speak of what binds them. Some complain—to themselves and to others. But only a few rise to action. And some, with heads lowered, do not even complain.

Action is not about rolling up your sleeves and getting to work. True action is the creation of authority—an authority that turns the impossible into the possible. Authority is aligning oneself with the intention of the world of meaning for a higher purpose.

Truth and Reality

The boundlessness of meaning—the more I comprehend it, the more I realize how limited our capabilities are on this journey of life. We possess almost nothing. We are utterly empty-handed. Yet, in our profound ignorance, we see ourselves as the center of existence. We are desperately empty-handed and heartbreakingly vulnerable.

Almost every day, I assess myself; the greatest losses stem from the things I believe in. In truth, it is because I have chosen to believe in them. Otherwise, they would be as inconsequential as the things I don't believe in.

There are very few things—if "existence" is even the right word—that I have convinced myself are worth believing. That is, I have accepted their existence and chosen to trust my perception of them. Yet, even this belief is not fixed. I cannot, for example, define my friends based on this perception or this belief in any steadfast or enduring way. I see that they change constantly and are not the same beings they were moments before.

Imagine I believe in a river; yet, nothing about that river is what it was a moment ago. That previous perception, that prior image, that earlier entity—no matter how tangible or believable it might have seemed—has completely flowed away with the movement of the water and been entirely transformed. In the face of this constant, dreamlike flux, this ceaseless and uninterrupted becoming and changing, I find it impossible to maintain a stable exchange with the environment and everything occurring within it. At best, I strive to present a fixed essence of myself.

This effort is rooted in the belief that if a perception similar to mine exists on the other side, then the receptors of that perception might grasp something consistent for as long as my perception remains constant. Unfortunately, I must admit that this behavior has yielded no benefit. In truth, a mutual understanding born of a stable perception, upon which some form of exchange could be established, never materializes.

In reality, I, too, am intermittently inconsistent or different from what my interlocutor believes me to be. That is, beyond the frameworks of our epistemological foundations in ordinary social life—which seem to be clearly defined—we have very little chance of encountering each other's true selves. At best, we encounter fleeting glimpses of a fluid essence, each time meeting a different aspect of it.

Put simply, if there were no drastic changes in what or who perceives itself as "me"—though such changes do exist—it would still perceive "me" as a different entity than it did a moment, a day, or a year ago. All of us are perceived by one another as being contrary to the expected perception of the preceding moment. A father does not fully comprehend his child, nor does a close friend truly understand their closest companion. We usually endure this lack of comprehension until the last glimmer of hope for genuine understanding is extinguished.

To put it more simply: we are all of one essence. The rapid pace of change within us creates this empty illusion, this baseless belief, that we are encountering something else. But until we come to perceive a tangible understanding of ourselves, we will neither understand anything nor anyone else.

We play discordant notes in the symphony of existence—unless, in a moment of selfless surrender, we move in harmony with the gentle melody of the instrument that joins the great symphony.

Order and Disorder

To be without questions, to lack inquiry, and to embody nothing but answers—to become the all-knowing—is not the end of the path. Meanings can arise even from the absence of questions. Without inquiry, without desire, and unexpectedly, meaning can bloom for something of which we had no prior conception— whether or not we had a question or any knowledge or understanding of it. It is knowledge beyond all logical systems of comprehension. In such a state, one encounters pure chaos, and yet, from its depths, something orderly suddenly emerges—without reason or any particular logic.

Things are always brought into order that cause a restless repetition in human beings—sometimes born of joy, sometimes sorrow, sometimes ecstasy, and other times apathy. To be orderly means that none of these can disrupt your inner equilibrium. It means remaining unmoved, as though a pebble were cast into an ocean too vast and turbulent to be affected by it. If you achieve this and truly know it, you will no longer be an easy prey for those who drain your energy.

To those who ask, "What should we do?" I say, "Align yourself with something orderly!" Our reactive behaviors have distorted us. Becoming orderly sometimes manifests as pure disorder. This may be hard to believe, but the world around us works in just such a way.

They ask, "How do we align ourselves with something orderly?" I reply, "If you look closely, you will see that there have been things striving to align you with them."

The first step is to free yourself from these forces. Without freeing yourself from them, you will not be able to choose.

Once you liberate yourself from all external aligners, you will discover your breath and heartbeat—those fundamental regulators that enable humans to perceive the material world with precision. The next step is to find what regulates even these two. You must take control of that regulator to align yourself with something greater.

Without sufficient energy, this task is impossible. Hidden or apparent, material or immaterial, there is only one truly valid force of alignment. Where you are and how you are connected to this force determines everything. When connected to this force, you may appear to exist in pure chaos—disorderly, unpredictable, and amidst pervasive tumult. This is the nature of that force; it may appear this way.

If the birth of the universe came from a great explosion, is an explosion an orderly phenomenon? Can an orderly universe emerge from a chaotic explosion? Our logic fails to explain the behaviors of this force.

To be orderly does not mean adhering to specific habits. It is not about meticulously planning every hour of the day. Orderliness is like the art of a martial arts master— prepared for any attack at any moment, nearly impossible to catch off guard, and capable of responding to every move with precise alignment. Orderliness is like a cat that lands on its feet no matter how it falls—at least in most cases, it is in control of itself. Someone whose habits are rigidly predictable, who drinks from a specific spring at the same time each day, is easy prey for a hunter who knows their routines. There is always an undeniable difference between habit and true order.

Awareness on the Path

Some believe that the ignorant bear no sorrow, while the weight of the world rests on the shoulders of the aware. Yet I tell you, the greatest sorrow is to lack awareness. If this assumption is wrong, then even still, it is better to grieve consciously than to rejoice in ignorance.

Moments arise when one falters, kneeling under the weight of the journey, yearning to abandon the path. A thousand reasons may surface, each more compelling than the last, to justify giving up. At times, the urge to leave is so overpowering that nothing can restrain it— nothing except a particular clarity: the unmistakable understanding that outside this path, there is truly nothing to be found.

A seeker knows that beyond this journey lies only monotony, stagnation, and decay. At the crossroads of struggle and comfort, I choose struggle. Without hesitation, the path constantly presents me with gifts— enticements meant to tempt me into embracing ease and forsaking this difficult journey. Yet, I reject these gifts and choose struggle; I was not created to be enslaved. We either strive to perfect our awareness or willingly surrender our energy to another being. There is no third way.

Human beings dream while asleep, experiencing visions both fleeting and profound. Dreams dissipate, but visions can manifest into reality. Likewise, seekers harbor illusions and imaginings. Illusions are wasted, while imaginings can shape reality. Illusions may be fabricated with smoke or drugs, but not imagination, which is pure and sacred, nourished by the wellspring of meaning. Some of my closest companions have heard of my imaginings and later bore witness as they came to life.

Just as sheep entrust themselves to their shepherd, following his voice, his movements, and his guidance, humans, too, are caught in the grasp of their captors. What a deep sorrow it is to fully comprehend this—to realize that the shepherd cultivates us only to harvest us. Meanwhile, wolves, hyenas, and leopards raid the flock of our existence. We, defenseless and helpless, drift away from the cycle of meaning. In this state, we even compete to become something else, tossed about by the waves of an ocean that sees us as no more than a straw. Overturned and submerged, we hope for another chance, another pure manifestation to rediscover ourselves. And when we are found again, the process of refinement begins anew within that vast ocean... only to realize, once more, that we are nothing—nothing at all.

The realm of meaning is an infinite ocean of awareness, perpetually birthing fresh creation, pouring itself forth to bring forth existence. Whoever truly grasps this will have only one aim in life: to align themselves with this pure current. This alignment requires no struggle—like lying effortlessly afloat on water. Meaning is the creator of both the tangible and intangible. It reveals itself through words, yet beyond words, it is apprehended directly. However, such understanding, when it transcends the senses, is proportional to one's level of awareness. It cannot be taught or learned. The more one comprehends meaning, the more they harmonize with creation. As this harmony deepens, their soul becomes ever more awake, eternal, and undying.

Know this: the universe is one, and if anything, whether visible or invisible, were to fall out of its orbit, all would collapse. What we perceive as separate stems only from our ignorance. One who truly knows will see themselves and all existence as one. Even that notion of floating, which I mentioned, ultimately dissolves—it, too, is an illusion.

The one who floats has become one with the water. But the one who perceives themselves as separate grows greedy for what they consider "other" and grasps at it to preserve their existence. Such a person cannot remain afloat, for they claw at everything in desperation, and without guidance, they sink further.

Beyond this world lies the indescribable realm of meaning, for which no description suffices. This is because that realm is pure awareness, and we lack even a drop of that awareness to comprehend it. All that appears—whether tangible or intangible—arises as a manifestation of that indescribable realm. That realm is like an ocean that pours itself out from its depths to create a new, only to draw itself back within.

In the balanced manifestations of that ineffable realm, there is no corruption. Corruption, in this sense, means fragmentation, separation. Yet nothing is truly fragmented; where there is wholeness, there is no lack, only completeness. But on our limited scale, whenever a person seeks possession, claiming something as their own and striving to preserve it, they isolate a minuscule fragment of the greater whole. They clutch at it, trying to keep it, but this act of grasping creates disharmony. On this scale, it is observable: the earth and sea seem to turn away from humanity, but in truth, it is humanity that turns away from itself.

Belief in lack—paired with the misguided effort to fix it using knowledge distant from true completeness—often leads one in the opposite, erroneous direction. And so, signs appear to remind us of our unity with the whole, and we find ourselves dissolving into it once again. These processes are not confined to the bounds of time. They can occur in an instant or unfold over millennia, for the essence of humanity transcends apparent death.

Wherever a person finds themselves trapped, it is the result of ignorance or self-imposed isolation, or of dissonant attachments in their environment. The path to liberation is to release—to empty oneself, to free oneself from corruption. If one cannot find freedom through letting go, then no other effort will suffice.

It is akin to the play of children. They see a toy, desire it, cry until they obtain it, but once it is abandoned, they return to joy and laughter, leaping about with no memory of their earlier longing. And when the mother hides the toy, the child's sorrow and longing mirror, on a smaller scale, the grief, famine, and injustices of the world. The toys of children differ from year to year, age to age. But the mother desires the child's uninhibited playfulness, for it connects to that indescribable realm.

Until you come to know yourself, you cannot understand what lies beyond yourself. And as long as you are entangled in your own self, knowing yourself is impossible. You must step outside yourself, view yourself from a distance, to illuminate your origin, your dwelling, and your destination. Split yourself in two: one half that observes and the other half that is observed. One half is of clay, and the other of spirit. When the heart half comprehends the state of the clay half, the clay will in turn recognize the heart. It will understand that the heart is the sanctuary of the soul, and the soul is something confined within specific boundaries of the heart, which itself is enclosed by the limits of the clay.

Paradise lies within you. "Within" is but a metaphor to convey that nothing exists in the external. Even the certainties of physics and mathematics are built upon assumptions, which, if altered, dissolve everything that rests upon them. As long as the mind remains occupied with constructing and describing the external world, that inner paradise will not reveal itself.

As long as the mind is influenced by acquired indoctrinations and continues along the repetitive paths of habit, there is no way to break free from the cage. Interpretations, such as the idea of a creator continuously observing every moment of existence, are merely attempts to rationalize being. Logic pertains only to the material, tangible world we inhabit. Do not spend your time on it. In another arrangement of awareness, the current logic we hold as infallible would dissolve into nothingness.

Human beings have always asked repetitive questions about the reason for their existence, and the customary answers seem almost ingrained in our genetic makeup. This historical inheritance is one of the greatest obstacles to truly understanding existence. It is a veil that requires courage and determination to tear apart, and the reward for doing so far outweighs the effort it demands.

Amid the forces surrounding me, I am so insignificant that I cannot even claim to exist. All I know is that a meaning flows through me, creating an illusory distinction between myself and my surroundings. This force of differentiation, in its essence, wields immense power against the overwhelmingly mighty forces around me, forming the separate identity I perceive as "me." This force is so powerful that whenever I am in complete connection with it, everything else becomes utterly insignificant. How extraordinary are the forces that can sever us from this empowering whole and intoxicate us with their allure!

Crossing the boundaries of awareness at different levels is like a meticulously planned military operation. Every ounce of energy must be at its peak. Anything that could diminish the capabilities of the seeker must be treated with the utmost seriousness. Just as a failed military operation, when compromised, can cost soldiers their lives, a failure to cross a threshold of awareness can lead to the loss of the seeker's essence or cause severe psychological fragmentation. At the very least, it will result in prolonged regression, leaving the seeker disheartened and desperate.

Many sudden mental illnesses stem from accidental encounters with the outer edges of human perception. Without actively pursuing a path, some individuals may inadvertently find themselves within the boundaries of these thresholds due to an unexpected event, leading to potential consequences.

Passing beyond the ordinary levels of perception erases the seeker's human form—not in the sense of physical appearance or abilities, but in the transformation of human emotions. After such a passage, the seeker can only feign human emotions. They permanently relinquish genuine human feelings, sometimes resorting to artful pretense to display them.

Interruptions in the continuity of human perception make it impossible to describe the surrounding world. If we comprehend the world around us, it is due to an uninterrupted flow of perception. When crossing the boundaries of ordinary human perception, maintaining precision within a specific level becomes the most challenging task. Without stability at a defined level, the seeker experiences ambiguous perceptions that quickly shift into another incoherent awareness.

Losing the human form without a solid anchor can leave the seeker adrift in the vast expanse of non-ordinary perceptions. Vigilance is essential. According to this understanding, the seeker requires a lifeline to return to ordinary human perception unless they choose to completely abandon this level of awareness.

Our outward senses—the five we rely upon—though obstacles to accessing higher levels of perception, are also the most reliable anchors for returning to ordinary perception. However, retaining even a small lifeline as an anchor presents a significant flaw: it makes focusing on and sustaining new levels of perception exceedingly difficult. Balancing between these two states requires the seeker to maintain maximum awareness.

Many mistakenly equate the spiritual path with methods of soothing the nerves. Yet the path of spiritual pursuit is a ceaseless, unrelenting battle—not one aimed at victory but at achieving the most refined way of being. A warrior either acts with the utmost precision or perishes. A spiritual journey that does not culminate in eternity is nothing but the foolish fantasy of a deluded mind. The path to immortality is entirely different from the path of pacifying the soul. A true spiritual journey may unsettle you more profoundly than anything else. How could this elixir of restlessness align with calming one's nerves?

The tranquility sought by seekers is neither small nor quickly attainable. This peace resembles the vastness of an ocean—deep, immense, and infinite—one that even seas cannot fathom. True peace arises only when the boundaries of one's restlessness are shattered. The spiritual journey is not even akin to a broken ship; it is merely a piece of driftwood amidst the sea. Peace and stability are meaningless without turmoil. And for years, humanity has deceived itself into believing it is stable in this world!

On the Nature of Humanity

To be human is profoundly terrifying when you realize where you stand. Yet, to be human is magnificently glorious when you understand that within you lies the power to create any reality. Today's human being, shrouded in a veil of forgetfulness, remains oblivious to both truths.

The accumulation of our life's experiences—from the moment of birth to this very instant—has led to the formation of a fictitious identity, which we call "self." Every time we speak, we refer to this constructed self. However, not even a single moment of this so-called "history" has any real existence. Despite this, we burden ourselves with the weight of its nonexistent emotions and carry them like heavy chains.

Feelings of guilt, failure, and the disappointments of the past cling to this fictional history, holding our freedom and presence in the moment hostage. On the other hand, another empty facet of this history serves as the source of our pride and boasts, constructing the false ego that traps us in its grip.

If our achievements were so great as to surpass those of the entire world, we could only claim victory if we freed ourselves from all attachments tied to those accomplishments. The greater these attachments relative to the achievements, the harder, and eventually impossible, it becomes to achieve liberation. Eliminating this illusory history and floating freely in the present moment is a Herculean task on the spiritual path.

Throughout my life, I have only rarely observed people, usually intoxicated or out of their senses, who, for a brief moment, were freed from this bondage. I can confidently say that I have never encountered anyone who intentionally and consciously escaped this trap. This inability is the primary reason why seekers on the path of spiritual journeying often bang their heads against walls of despair. They are unwilling to let go of their nonexistent past and their false pride.

Time and again, friends and close ones have reproached me for my indifference and carelessness toward what has already occurred. Yet, for me, the past has no existential reality. Neither sorrow, nor regret, nor any grounds for pride or ego exist in moments that have passed. I have already discussed the nature of human pride in an earlier chapter.

The nature of this world is not as we interpret it. The idea that "I am me, and you are you, and that hunter is the hunter, and this shepherd is the shepherd"—this perception stems from a gap in our understanding. It is this unavoidable division that allows us to distinguish ourselves. When you are you, then I become me.

The tangible world we experience is shaped through vibrations. By manipulating these vibrations, we can alter the form of the world. To create a desired vibration, one requires a force that can be called willpower. The root of this will lies in inner energy, and attaining inner energy demands discipline and perseverance.

In higher states of perception, other sensory dimensions become apparent—dimensions that cannot be grasped by our usual five senses. Each time we insist on clinging to the certainty of our sensory understanding, we engage in a profoundly foolish act. We see shadows cast long ago, which bear no resemblance to the true nature of what created them. Yet, we naively trust our sensory perception and confidently accept its illusions.

In the infinite ocean of meaning, only the currents of awareness are in motion. I compete with you, bending my neck to the blade of a hunter who is of the same essence as you and me. This hunter is us, yet exists on another plane of awareness. All that occurs is the interplay of awareness, manifesting as the undulating waves of this boundless ocean—an ocean without beginning or end, entirely of one substance.

It is a singularity that pours itself from its own depths, shaping itself into diverse forms and dreams. It becomes tangible to each perception according to what that perception can comprehend, yet, in its essence, it is none of these forms or meanings. It eludes all understanding and resists being defined.

We perceive the contradictions of this world, but beyond this point, our senses fall deaf, blind, and mute. For a seeker, it is better to embrace joy so that the meaning of sorrow can also be illuminated—or to uproot the source of both, leaving no sorrow and no joy. How could one long for someone if there were no such thing as fulfillment to begin with? When these feelings are uprooted, something new emerges.

When my heart longs for someone, I realize it is because they are longing for me—because longing no longer belongs to me; it is no longer mine.

Human beings are astonishingly complex, and the universe around them is even more intricate. I witness things but cannot understand them. I understand things but cannot express them. Over the years, as the circumference of my observations has widened, my understanding of existence has diminished. In the face of this vast expanse, I seem to know nothing.

My understanding was like a juggler, keeping two balls spinning in the air with one hand. But now my observation perceives billions of jugglers, each juggling billions of balls, all spinning together. The balls, the juggling, the jugglers—all in motion! Understanding, observation, and the observer—all in motion! It is maddening, indescribable.

We speak to ourselves, and we hear ourselves, unaware of the myriad things there are to truly hear. The world around us is a grand symphony, with musicians playing in every corner. One must learn to listen.

Humanity is a strange being. Within every human lies a dormant beast. When awakened, nothing can restrain it. There are times when this beast awakens collectively, as if roused from a deep hibernation. Humanity is capable of taking another's life. Humanity is capable of bringing another to their knees without ending their life. Yet, between these two extremes, a subtle space exists.

A person brought to their knees, with their helplessness laid bare, if left in that state, can become a source of immense power—power that transcends the logic of the material world. In their severance from all attachments, a concentration arises within them that mirrors the culmination of a lifetime of spiritual seeking. What they will in this state may come to pass.

Never place anyone in such a condition, and never find satisfaction in another's helplessness, for it can transform into their ultimate strength, turning everything upside down. This is a warning to anyone who wields power—whether a person over another or a ruler over a nation.

Humans often tie their survival and legacy to the eternal. This is how countless gods of many colors and forms have been born.

The human who once worshiped stone, wood, or stars is equally capable of worshiping other things—other humans, even imaginary gods. But I tell you with certainty: nothing is truly worthy of worship. There is no sanctity in anything. Whatever it is—no matter how sacred—holds no greater value than those idols of stone.

Beware! The imagined geography of heavenly paradises often lies beside the inferno of ignorance. The system of punishment and reward is effective only in taming animal instincts. Breaking free from the cycle of imposed habits is the gateway to the realm of meaning. And the realm of meaning is the realm of awareness—not punishment or reward!

The growth of meaning in a human is not rooted in their physicality but in the way they connect to meaning. Most of us, even after years, remain like infants—crying endlessly for milk. That is how I see the greed of this world. But I have been weaned; I am free. I can consume all things, and yet, I hunger for nothing. Some are like this—they consume everything, but they are not ravenous for the world.

Weaning a child from milk is difficult. Mothers often make the milk bitter so the child will no longer desire it—so they will let go. And letting go is tied to not wanting: with or without reason, through trickery or other means, there is always a path to freedom. The spiritual growth of a human mirrors this process. The smallness of humanity in the vast cosmos does not preclude its infinite potential.

I saw a tiny seed that had grown into a mighty tree. I spoke to it. It said, "No seed can ever comprehend the magnitude of a tree." It explained, "There is something shared in the nowhere—a knowing that seeds understand without ever knowing why."

I told it, "Humans are the same. The more they learn, the greater their ignorance grows. And no one will ever emerge who can truly understand it all, let alone know it." Then I said, "At least trees are better. They don't ask questions and aren't led astray by answers. They have no teachers or students to entangle them in the endless loop of trying to explain the inexplicable. They simply grow or don't, and either way, they bear no grief."

An angel standing against a devil must remember that the devil was once an angel too. A human standing against a devil possesses far greater potential for devilry than even the devil itself! There are places where boundaries are not just thin as a hair—they are completely intertwined. I have crawled through these shared borders, moving from disbelief to faith, from light to darkness, from home to ruin, and back again.

What I share is no fable; it is lived experience. Harsh, grueling, and relentless experience, where you must give everything you have to gain something new, only to find that this new thing, too, is dissolving, eroding, and fading just as intensely as what came before.

Our work is to be restless—not because I say so, but because the path of love is one of madness, of disarray, until it leads to the final resting place: Layla's sanctuary, and nowhere else.

"The Beloved desires this restlessness;
Better futile effort than slumbering stillness.
Carve and chisel away on this path;
Until the final breath, never rest." – Rumi

When asked, "What did you see in this calamity?" the response was: "I saw nothing but beauty." The more a witness perceives, the less choice they seem to have—not in the sense of desiring but being unable, but rather in being utterly incapable of even desiring. Perhaps it's better to say, they want nothing. They don't even want to want.

Love

The longing for physical presence and connection among humans, like all material desires, stems from the instinct for survival.

The formation of human societies, individual relationships, and even the concept of love between two people—all are ultimately mechanisms to ensure survival. These instincts are reinforced by sweet hormonal and chemical rewards that have been ingrained in us over centuries.

Although cloaked in noble terms like love, altruism, or other ethical virtues, such relationships are, at their core, physical and mechanical processes that secure the continuity of human existence.

Lost halves, unfulfilled lovers, the poetry of longing, the ecstasy and sorrow of love—all these only find meaning within the framework of that same goal: the preservation of human life.

I provide this prelude to clarify a different type of relationship. When the material drive for survival fades while traversing spiritual peaks, the games rooted in physical preservation lose their significance. When the conversation turns to eternity, the struggle for material survival and its attachments becomes so trivial that it is hardly worth discussing.

The question arises: can a relationship exist between two individuals at this stage? If so, what is its foundation, and what is its focus, now that physical survival is no longer a concern?

If I were to name this connection, I would call it "becoming one soul." I say "becoming" because this state does not tolerate duality. It is akin to the hidden yearning within the branches of a tree—though they grow in different directions, they all trace back to a single root.

This connection creates an opportunity for infinite eternity to establish and extend its rule. I see meaning through the other's eyes, and they hear through my ears. These are not concepts that can be explained to a person trapped in the hatchery of survival, whose sole aim is to fulfill the desires of their captors.

True love is not an exchange; it is not transactional. To love is to give; it is to sacrifice—freely and without expectation. In typical relationships, both parties usually enter with the intent to take, not to give.

Maternal love may be a good example of this concept. This is not to suggest that it is one-sided love. One-sided love is incomplete and does not reach fulfillment. What I mean is a mindset focused on giving, not on receiving; thus, even the smallest return feels like an immense blessing. A child's smile can feel like it compensates for everything to a mother.

How can we believe that the same hand that gives pain also offers healing unless pain and healing are one and the same? The beloved and the healer seem to embody opposites, yet their essence is unified. Pain comes from both the beloved and the healer, as does healing.

We willingly endure the blade of the healer because we trust in the cure. Yet, we flee from the beloved's frown because we expect tenderness.

Our measures are strange. We interpret one thing in several contradictory ways. We constrict the world around us! There is no pain. There is no cure. We construct illusions to sustain the world. We see our reflection in the water and fail to recognize it.

We are afraid. From our fears, we weave tales—creating gods, devils, demons, and angels within our stories—and then we believe them.

Contrary to these apparent dualities, the saints of the unseen realm are unified in meaning. Whatever form they manifest in, their essence is one. Thus, the fire of Abraham will not burn him. The staff of Moses is a sign, splitting the Nile to bring forth blossoms and, when necessary, becoming a serpent. Be a serpent if you are in Moses' hand, and witness that from the bottom of a well to the throne of a king, the path of Josephs is one known only to themselves.

No one, relying solely on their own awareness, can find their way to the state of this drunken sanctuary. The coordinates of that state are mapped on a different axis. Yet, it is impossible to measure this state from within it!

Love, as it is celebrated, was not what it seemed!
It broke our bones!

We mocked the endurance of rocks,
But love broke our bones!
We sought tenderness in love,
It was pure cruelty, sheer brutality!
It broke our bones!
We turned to truth, but it paraded as illusion!
It defied us so completely,
It broke our bones!
(Gholamreza Rashidi)

So, do not call those who do not stake their lives as collateral for love "lovers," for this path is one of those who carry their souls in their hands. It is the realm of the fearless, the sanctuary of those who have pledged their very being in surrender to the ever-increasing demands of love.

The Goddess (Woman)

Those who speak of the equality of men and women neither understand women nor men... They only see appearances, and even seeing leads nowhere.

When I speak of the goddess of women, I am not speaking of gender. I am trying to convey an impossible meaning—one that, within the spiritual identity of manhood, is almost entirely ungraspable.

The spiritual literature of my homeland revolves around the beloved as a woman. The beloved is the goddess.

This is not because this literature was created by men, but because those men were graced by the favor of goddesses (women).

It doesn't matter what belief you hold about a god. Just imagine for a moment that you are standing face-to-face with a god!

What remains of you? What notion could you possibly have of such an event? Annihilation occurs in an instant—the very annihilation that a seeker may strive for an entire lifetime to achieve, or fail to achieve.

The goddesses surround me—and you as well...

Wherever I turn...

Blessing is the act of creation, of giving life. It is the antithesis of misfortune. The goddess is blessed because she is a creator. Her ability to give birth does not diminish her; perfection is not reduced, and there is no misfortune in it.

Wealth is not perfection, for sharing it diminishes it. But sharing knowledge increases it. This is blessing. Thus, if wealth grows through giving, they say it is blessed—it holds barakah.

Woman is blessed in this way: even if misfortune befalls her, it too becomes blessed.

A dog may dip its muzzle into the ocean, yet the ocean is not diminished.

I speak of the whole; do not bring me examples of the partial.

The identity of the goddess is rooted in grace, not in need. Where blessing exists, there is no need. From within herself, through her repeated acts of creation, eternal self-sufficiency emerges.

The masculine identity is fire—it must burn something. This is an eternal need.

Creation, grace, and need weave the cycle of meaning into being. Those who wish to see the goddess as needy are at war with meaning. But no one can win a war against meaning. Meaning gives birth to timelessness, while its challengers are bound by the limits of time.

The birthing goddess is connected to meaning; she is meaning, taking one of countless unparalleled forms. In this realm, meaning takes the form of a fertile tool. The tree is a tool for creation, water is a tool for creation, the sun is a tool for creation. Yet the goddess is not the tree, nor the water, nor the sun.

The goddess gives birth to all things. She gives birth to trees, to the sun. The goddess is not afraid to give birth to demons, nor to need. Despite her essence being rooted in grace, she gives birth to need!

This world, drowning in need, was created in this way—nurtured by the goddesses of grace. Their desired creation was need, and so they bore it!

The birthing goddess is unafraid to be singular or manifold. I saw a goddess manifesting in thousands. Wherever you see a woman creating—even a man creating—it is one of the countless faces of a single goddess.

I saw a goddess painting,
I saw a goddess composing poetry,
I saw a goddess giving birth to silence!

Once, people revered a goddess for every element of existence, each one the sovereign ruler over its realm: the goddess of water, the goddess of rain, the goddess of the sea, and so forth.

Just as women give birth to men, goddesses gave birth to prophets—and also to devils. Prophets of devils and devils of prophets, locked in their needy conflict, were cast far from their nurturing mothers. A child who flees from their mother finds no lasting purpose. A mischievous child may stumble and wound themselves, but the birthing mother is untroubled—she can birth again. Her time is infinite, boundless. The entire drama of fire-wielding prophets barely spans a few thousand years.

Today's devout barely comprehend their prophets, let alone the goddesses. They know nothing of goddesses and still harm women!

The prophets are dead. The goddesses remain beyond the reach of ordinary understanding. Yet women... women... women remain the only precious gift that connects the material to the spiritual. Blessed are the women who inherit this priceless treasure!

I do not speak of gender. I want you to understand that there is a place where everything exists, a place devoid of need—a place that has everything, except need!

This place is self-evident in its grace. If you intend to journey there, bring with you what it lacks. It does not care for your grace; it does not desire it. What it lacks, however, is your need. It does not matter whether you are a man or a woman—if you carry need, it is easy to prove. A person in need has no pride.

If pride remains, it means you are still lingering...

Fear

Ignorance gives birth to fear. The unknown is terrifying. This is the first fear, one that everyone can understand. We fear the darkness because we do not know what lies within it. This lack of knowledge, this fear, is often used as a tool of deception—fear of something that might not even exist. Know this: any path that thrives on fear to advance itself is a path built on unconscious belief. Awareness lights the way and dispels fear.

There is also a second fear. This fear is born from knowledge, and only a few ever experience it. A human being is the continuation of awareness in time—created anew in every moment, unfolding moment by moment. If this continuous creation were to stop, even for an instant, awareness would be severed from the body. This accumulation of awareness would then dissipate into the realm of meaning, becoming lost—unless one has learned how to perceive oneself without the tools of the body.

In dreams, one experiences something and gains an understanding of it. Yet upon waking, one realizes that everything comprehended in the dream was nothing. It cannot be said that nothing was perceived—something was, but upon waking, that understanding no longer exists; it becomes void.

Our waking state is much the same. In another perception, all of it—everything we know—becomes void. Our tangible world, no matter how frightening or beautiful, is a persistent illusion that ends with death.

From another perspective, fear begins in us when the boldness of childhood fades, when we believe ourselves to be wise and view the world analytically rather than with curiosity and wonder.

And yet, the entire drama of the world is but a child's game—at times it makes us laugh, at other times it leaves us battered and bruised.

Many of the things we fear will never happen, and many of the things we long for will also never come to pass.

There is a middle path, a narrow line that forms the reality of our lives. This line holds a handful of joys and the usual difficulties.

But often, because of our fixation on the impossible, we fail to truly grasp what is possible.

It matters little what social, cultural, or economic class we belong to—most of us spend our precious lives lost between what is and what is not.

We often come to understand the right concepts far too late—the same principles that we've based our misguided decisions on throughout life.

One must have certainty that this world, down to its most fundamental elements, is balanced. Wherever imbalance arises, it is corrected.

Injustice is nothing but imbalance, born of excess or deficiency.

If we do not restore this imbalance ourselves, the structure of the universe will restore it.

The soul of a human being is a precious weight in the scales of humanity. If, out of fear for your life, you tolerate oppression, know that the universe will claim your soul to restore that balance!

Are you waiting for a devastating reckoning?

Then I promise it will come to you the moment you bow your head to a tyrant out of fear!